THE CHRISTMAS STORY

BASED ON THE GOSPELS ACCORDING TO SAINT MATTHEW AND SAINT LUKE

Retold by Deborah Hautzig

Illustrated by Sheilah Beckett

Random House 🏠 New York

LONG AGO in the city of Nazareth there lived a carpenter named Joseph and his wife, Mary. They had a small house, and they had a donkey, but they did not have any children.

One day when Mary was alone in the garden, an
angel appeared. It was the angel Gabriel. Mary did
not know why Gabriel had come, and she was afraid.

"Do not be afraid, Mary," the angel said. "You
are special and favored by God, and he has chosen

you to be the mother of his son. Your son's name
will be Jesus. He will be born a king and his
kingdom will never end.''

Mary was very happy.

When it was almost time for Mary to have her baby, Joseph said, "We must take a trip to Bethlehem to pay our taxes. It is a long journey, but you can ride our donkey." And so they went.

When Mary and Joseph came to Bethlehem, it was late at night and they were very tired. But there was no room for them at the inn. The innkeeper said they could sleep in the stable, so they went there to rest for the night.

In the stable were a cow, a lamb, a goat, and a dove. The animals were friendly. They let Joseph and Mary use their hay for a bed.

That very night, Mary's child was born. She wrapped him in soft cloth to keep him warm. There was no crib for the baby, so Mary laid him in the animals' manger.

In the fields outside of Bethlehem, shepherds watched over their flocks of sheep. Suddenly a light appeared in the night sky. The shepherds looked up and saw an angel. They were afraid until the angel spoke.

"I am bringing you news of great joy," said the angel. "Tonight in the city of Bethlehem, a savior has been born. He is called Jesus Christ, and he is our Lord. You will find the baby wrapped in swaddling clothes, lying in a manger."

The shepherds went to Bethlehem. When they found the stable, they were filled with joy at the sight of the child and knelt beside the manger to honor him. Then they went out to tell people what the angel had said about the newborn baby.

Far away in the East lived three wise men named Caspar, Melchior, and Balthazar, who had watched the skies for many years. They knew that someday a new star would rise to announce the birth of their king.

At last it appeared—a bright, glowing star they had never seen before.

The wise men set out to follow the star. They traveled westward across many miles of desert. The star was their guide. It led them to Bethlehem. Then it came to rest right above a little stable.

The wise men entered the stable, and when they saw the baby they knew they had found their king.

They gave him gifts of gold and wonderfully scented perfumes, frankincense and myrrh.

The wise men worshiped the child as the shepherds had, and they rejoiced.

Even the animals in the stable knew how special this baby was. Everyone knew he would be kind and gentle. They knew he would be a wise teacher, and a friend to all animals and to all people.

And he was. Every year at Christmas time, we celebrate the birth of Jesus Christ, because he brought the good news of God's love to all living things.